W9-CKC-808

God's Word: A Never-Failing Remedy

God's Word: A Never-Failing Remedy

Kenneth E. Hagin

Unless otherwise indicated, all Scripture quotations in this volume are from the *King James Version* of the Bible.

First Printing 1997

ISBN 0-89276-526-7

In the U.S. write:
Kenneth Hagin Ministries
P.O. Box 50126
Tulsa, OK 74150-0126

In Canada write:
Kenneth Hagin Ministries
P.O. Box 335, Station D,
Etobicoke (Toronto), Ontario
Canada, M9A 4X3

Copyright © 1997 RHEMA Bible Church
AKA Kenneth Hagin Ministries, Inc.
All Rights Reserved
Printed in USA

The Faith Shield is a trademark of RHEMA Bible Church, AKA Kenneth Hagin Ministries, Inc., registered with the U.S. Patent and Trademark Office and therefore may not be duplicated.

BOOKS BY KENNETH E. HAGIN

* *Redeemed From Poverty, Sickness and Spiritual Death*
* *What Faith Is*
* *Seven Vital Steps To Receiving the Holy Spirit*
* *Right and Wrong Thinking*
  Prayer Secrets
* *Authority of the Believer (foreign only)*
* *How To Turn Your Faith Loose*
  The Key to Scriptural Healing
  Praying To Get Results
  The Present-Day Ministry of Jesus Christ
  The Gift of Prophecy
  Healing Belongs to Us
  The Real Faith
  How You Can Know the Will of God
  The Threefold Nature of Man
  The Human Spirit
  Turning Hopeless Situations Around
  Casting Your Cares Upon the Lord
  Seven Steps for Judging Prophecy
* *The Interceding Christian*
  Faith Food for Autumn
* *Faith Food for Winter*
  Faith Food for Spring
  Faith Food for Summer
* *New Thresholds of Faith*
* *Prevailing Prayer to Peace*
* *Concerning Spiritual Gifts*
  Bible Faith Study Course
  Bible Prayer Study Course
  The Holy Spirit and His Gifts
* *The Ministry Gifts (Study Guide)*
  Seven Things You Should Know About Divine Healing
  El Shaddai
  Zoe: The God-Kind of Life
  A Commonsense Guide to Fasting
  Must Christians Suffer?
  The Woman Question
  The Believer's Authority
  Ministering to Your Family
  What To Do When Faith Seems Weak and Victory Lost
  Growing Up, Spiritually
  Bodily Healing and the Atonement (Dr. T.J. McCrossan)
  Exceedingly Growing Faith
  Understanding the Anointing
  I Believe in Visions
  Understanding How To Fight the Good Fight of Faith
  Plans, Purposes, and Pursuits
  How You Can Be Led by the Spirit of God
  A Fresh Anointing
  Classic Sermons
  He Gave Gifts Unto Men:
      A Biblical Perspective of Apostles, Prophets, and Pastors
  The Art of Prayer
  Following God's Plan For Your Life

The Triumphant Church: Dominion Over All the Powers of Darkness
Healing Scriptures
Mountain-Moving Faith
Love: The Way to Victory
Biblical Keys to Financial Prosperity
Jesus — The Open Door
The Price Is Not Greater Than God's Grace (Mrs. Oretha Hagin)

MINIBOOKS (A partial listing)

* *The New Birth*
* *Why Tongues?*
* *In Him*
* *God's Medicine*
* *You Can Have What You Say*
* *Don't Blame God*
* *How To Keep Your Healing*
  The Bible Way To Receive the Holy Spirit
  I Went to Hell
  How To Walk in Love
  The Precious Blood of Jesus
* *Love Never Fails*
  How God Taught Me About Prosperity

BOOKS BY KENNETH HAGIN JR.

* *Man's Impossibility — God's Possibility*
  Because of Jesus
  How To Make the Dream God Gave You Come True
  The Life of Obedience
  Forget Not!
  God's Irresistible Word
  Healing: Forever Settled
  Don't Quit! Your Faith Will See You Through
  The Untapped Power in Praise
  Listen to Your Heart
  What Comes After Faith?
  Speak to Your Mountain!
  Come Out of the Valley!
  It's Your Move!
  God's Victory Plan
  Another Look at Faith
  How To Live Worry-Free
  Soaring With the Eagles

MINIBOOKS (A partial listing)

* *Faith Worketh by Love*
* *Seven Hindrances to Healing*
* *The Past Tense of God's Word*
  Faith Takes Back What the Devil's Stolen
  How To Be a Success in Life
  Unforgiveness
  Ministering to the Brokenhearted

*These titles are also available in Spanish. Information about other foreign translations of several of the above titles (i.e., Finnish, French, German, Indonesian, Polish, Russian, etc.) may be obtained by writing to: Kenneth Hagin Ministries, P.O. Box 50126, Tulsa, Oklahoma 74150-0126.

Contents

Chapter 1
God's Word Is Medicine

My son, attend to my words; incline thine ear unto my sayings.

Let them not depart from thine eyes; keep them in the midst of thine heart.

For they are LIFE unto those that find them, and HEALTH to all their flesh.

— Proverbs 4:20-22

. . . the words that I speak unto you, THEY ARE SPIRIT, and THEY ARE LIFE.

— John 6:63

This verse in Proverbs tells exactly how to find the never-failing remedy for every problem you will ever face in life. It tells how you can have life and health.

That is the main thing people are seeking after — abundant life — which includes healing and health. All of God's blessings are found in His Word because it is a never-failing remedy.

God wants us to understand the life and power that are in His Word. When God made the world,

1

He created the earth, sky, and the great expanse of the universe with *words*. (*See* Genesis chapter 1.)

Therefore, God's Word has creative power because His words are *spirit* and they are *life*. *Therefore*, God's Word is a never-failing remedy for any situation or circumstance that might come your way in life, including sickness and disease.

You see, God's Word is God's medicine for your flesh. Proverbs 4:22 says God's words ". . . *are LIFE unto those that find them, and HEALTH to all their flesh.*" That means God's words are full of *life*, *health*, and *healing*.

God's words act like medicine. In fact, the margin of my Bible states that the word for "health" is *medicine*. Therefore, His words are medicine. Medicine for what? *For all your flesh!*

You could say it this way: "God's words are *words of life* and *words of health* for my body." But they are also words of life and words of health for any circumstance you may face in life. All of God's blessings are contained in His Word!

Attend to My Words

Notice that Proverbs 4:20 says, ". . . *attend to my WORDS.* . . ." That means *give God's Word your undivided attention*. In other words, put God's Word *into* your heart, and put out of your heart everything else that exalts itself against the Word.

Put out of your heart all the distractions that would rob you from giving the Word your full attention. Put the Word first.

One reason folks fail to receive *life* and *health* from God is that they don't find God's Word; they don't attend to it. But these verses say that if you will attend to God's Word or put it first, you will find life *and* health. That's quite a statement!

Incline Your Ears to My Sayings

The last part of Proverbs 4:20 says, ". . . *incline thine ear unto my sayings.*" That means take God's Word in through your ear gates. Open your ears to God's sayings. Drink His words in by hearing them.

However, when God said to incline your ear to His sayings, that means more than just hearing the Word once or twice. For example, people say, "Oh, I've heard that already."

But, you see, inclining your ear to God's sayings is a continual action. You are to be *continuously* hearing His Word. Keep your ears hearing and hearing the Word (Rom. 10:17).

If you are attending to God's Word and you are *opening* your ears to God's sayings, then you are *closing* your ears to all other sayings that would try to rob the Word from you, such as fear, doubt, and unbelief.

The Word can be life and health to all your flesh right now! All you have to do is take God's medicine — His Word — as your remedy. God's Word can be a remedy to any situation in your life. But first you will have to read and know it for yourself.

You can hear the Word quoted, but sometimes it can roll off you like water running off a duck's back and not register on your spirit. But if you will get the Word down on the inside of you and know for yourself what the Word of God says, it will begin to work for you.

You see, when you know that the Word of God is true, you'll not doubt it. You'll not take issue with the Word or take sides against it because it will be rooted deeply in your heart. Once it is in your heart, it is a never-failing remedy for the problems of life.

Don't Let My Word
Depart From Your Eyes

It is important what you *listen* to. Proverbs 4:20 tells you exactly what you should be listening to if you want life and health: *". . . incline thine ear unto MY SAYINGS."*

But it is also important what you *see* — what you set your eyes on — because the Bible says, *"Let them* [My Words] *not depart from THINE EYES . . ."* (Prov. 4:21). Therefore, you are supposed to *look* as well as *listen* to God's Word.

In other words, keep your vision fixed on God's Word. Keep your eyes fixed on Jesus and on the Word of God. Don't look at circumstances; look to the Word!

This Scripture doesn't mean we are to continually look at the Word so that we never do anything else. But it means we are to always look *to* the Word instead of *at* the circumstances. In the good times and in the bad, we just need to keep looking at God's words — at His sayings.

God's Word! Just keep looking at those words. Look at them so you can keep them where? In the midst of your *heart*! Why? Because then they will be life to *you*! They are words of life and health!

But notice that God's words are only life to those who find them: *". . . they are life unto those THAT FIND THEM. . . ."* Some people never find them because they never incline their ears to them! Other people never find God's words because they never attend to His Word or put it first. They put everything else first before God's sayings.

In days gone by, people used to travel primarily by train. Railroads crisscrossed this country. In those days, we didn't have all the lights and electronic equipment to mark train crossings like they do today. At railroad crossings, a sign would simply say, "Stop! Look! And listen!"

That is exactly what God's Word is saying in this passage of Scripture. If you want life and

health there is something *you* must do. *Stop.*
"Attend to My words." *Look.* "Let them not depart
from before thine eyes." *Listen.* "Incline your ear to
My sayings." In other words, s*top, look, and listen*
to God's Word.

Don't let God's words depart from before your
eyes. Why? Because absolutely tremendous results
can come forth as a result of having the Word continually before your eyes. The Word brings forth
results because God's words are life to those who
find them. They are health to *all* their flesh.

You see, it is so simple. If people would only
attend to God's Word, His Word would be health and
healing to them. God's Word contains words that are
like medicine because they are spirit and life
(John 6:63).

There's power in the Word! There is healing in
God's Word too. Notice Proverbs 4:22: "God's words
are . . . health. . . ." They can heal your flesh, no
matter what is wrong with you!

That means when you incline your ear to God's
words, the Word will be full of life, health, and
healing to all your flesh — to your *body* and anything else that ails you.

Incline Your Ear to God's Word — Not to Your Own Opinions

You are to incline your ear to God's Word
because God's Word has the power to heal your

body and set you free. You could say, "The Bible —
God's Word — is God personally speaking to me."

"Yes," someone said, "I know what the Bible says
about healing, but I don't believe it just that way."

If you have that attitude, you are not inclining
your ear to *God*'s sayings — to *His* Word. Instead,
you are inclining your ear to your own beliefs and
opinions.

One fellow said to me, "I've got just as much
right to my beliefs as you have to yours."

I answered him, "No, you don't and neither do I,
not if we want to prosper and walk in divine
health. If we want to prosper and have God's blessings in life, neither one of us has a right to our own
beliefs unless they line up with the Bible."

Some Christians don't incline their ears unto
God's sayings because they always want to hear
something *new* from the Word — some *new* revelation. The only problem is they haven't acted on the
revelation they already have about healing! They
haven't walked in the light of the Word they
already have!

So when someone preaches or teaches on sub-
jects like faith and healing, these Christians say,
"Oh, I've heard all that before." But those folks
aren't inclining their ears to God's sayings!

You see, the Word doesn't work for you just
because you *have inclined* your ear once or twice to
God's sayings. No, to incline your ear denotes an

ongoing, continual action. You've got to continually incline your ear to God's sayings for His Word to work for you.

Proverbs 4:20 and 22 says, *". . . incline thine ear unto my sayings. . . . For they are life unto those that find them, and health* [or medicine] *to all their flesh."*

How To Take Your Medicine

God's Word is medicine. That means it is a never-failing remedy for anything that ails you, including everything that pertains to your life. God's Word is a remedy for anything in your life that needs to be changed.

And since God's Word is medicine to all our flesh, how do we take God's medicine — His Word — and appropriate it for the healing of our bodies?

> **PROVERBS 4:20,21**
> **20 My son, ATTEND to my words; INCLINE thine ear unto my sayings.**
> **21 Let them NOT DEPART from thine eyes; KEEP them in the midst of thine heart.**

We take God's medicine by doing what Proverbs 4:20 and 21 says to do:

1. *Attend* to God's Word.

2. *Incline* your ear unto it.

3. *Let God's Word not depart* from your eyes.

4. *Keep it* in the midst of your heart.

All these instructions imply a continual, ongoing action, not something you do one time or every once in a while.

In the natural, suppose you had an illness last year, and your doctor prescribed a certain kind of medicine for you to take. Then suppose you got sick again this year with the same illness, and the doctor prescribed the same kind of medicine for you.

You wouldn't tell your doctor, "Oh, no, Doctor! I can't take that medicine. I took that *last* year!"

The medicine you took when you needed it last year isn't going to do you a bit of good if you need it again this year. If you need medicine now, you'll have to take it again before it can profit you.

It is the same way with God's Word; you have to keep on taking God's medicine for it to benefit you. You do the *inclining* and God will do the *healing* and *restoring*!

But God's Word won't benefit you if you have the attitude, *I've heard all that before.* No, in order for God's Word to do you any good, you have to stay with it. You've got to continually appropriate the healing power in God's medicine.

The Bible says faith is the victory: ". . . *this is the victory that overcometh the world, even our faith* (1 John 5:4). But faith comes by hearing the Word of God, not by *having heard* it (Rom. 10:17). Therefore, when you *keep on* hearing God's Word and you appropriate it for yourself, that's when it brings you victory!

Chapter 2
Jesus: The Will of God In Action

Have you ever struggled in certain areas of your life, wondering what the will of God was in your particular situation or circumstance? There is great peace and comfort in knowing the will of God.

The Psalmist of old said, *"How precious also are thy thoughts unto me, O God! how great is the sum of them!"* (Ps. 139:17).

How can you know the will of God in the situations and circumstances of life? By inclining your ear to God's sayings: *". . . attend to my words. . . . For they are life. . . and health . . ."* (Prov. 4:20,22).

God's *Word* is God's *will*, so when you know His Word and act on it, it brings you life and health!

Jesus' Ministry Demonstrated God's Will

Jesus' earthly ministry was the will of God in action on behalf of mankind. Jesus said in John 6:38, *". . . I came down from heaven, not to do mine own will, but the will of him that sent me."*

The Bible also says it is God's will for Jesus to heal all those who are oppressed by the devil. That includes those who are oppressed with sickness and disease.

ACTS 10:38
38 How God anointed Jesus of Nazareth with the Holy Ghost and with power: WHO WENT ABOUT DOING GOOD, and HEALING ALL THAT WERE OPPRESSED OF THE DEVIL; for God was with him.

Remember that Jesus came not to do His own will, but the will of Him who sent Him. With that thought in mind, remember that Jesus was carrying out God's will on the earth by doing good.

Is it good to heal people? Did Jesus do God's will when He went about healing all who were oppressed by the devil? Certainly He did.

Well, if Jesus was carrying out God's will on the earth by doing good and healing folks, then has God's will changed about healing people today who are oppressed by the devil?

Of course not, because the Bible says God never changes: *"For I am the Lord, I change not. . . "* (Mal. 3:6). Jesus is the same yesterday, today, and forever (Heb. 13:8).

Therefore, God's Word reveals to us that He never changes — even on the subject of healing. In other words, whatever He has done for anyone else, He will do for *you* if you will take Him at His Word and trust Him for it.

Since God doesn't change, we can know for certain that it is God's will to heal everyone. Actually, Acts 10:38 should be enough to convince us that it is God's will to heal today. But there are also many other verses that reveal to us God's will concerning healing.

That's why we need to incline our ears to God's Word — to His sayings — so His words can be life, health, and medicine to us.

God Speaks to Us Through Jesus

I've said before that the Bible — God's Word — is God speaking to each one of us personally. And Jesus' earthly ministry was the express will of God in action.

Jesus is God, the *Word* made flesh. Therefore, to know what God is saying to us, we have to know what the Word is saying to us.

JOHN 1:1,14
1 In the beginning was THE WORD, and THE WORD was with God, and THE WORD WAS GOD. . . .
14 And THE WORD WAS MADE FLESH, and dwelt among us, (and we beheld his glory, the glory as of the only begotten of the Father,) full of grace and truth.

Because Jesus is God, the Word made flesh, we can say that *Jesus* is God speaking to us personally. In fact, the Bible says that God speaks to us through Jesus, the living Word. And God's holy written Word contains the sayings of Jesus.

> **HEBREWS 1:1,2**
> **1 GOD, who at sundry times and in divers manners SPAKE in time past unto the fathers by the prophets,**
> **2 Hath in these last days SPOKEN UNTO US BY HIS SON, whom he hath appointed heir of all things, by whom also he made the worlds.**

Since Jesus is God speaking to us, I wonder what God is saying to us through Jesus? We need to incline our ears to everything Jesus says to us.

For example, when Jesus went about doing good and healing all who were oppressed of the devil, I wonder what He was saying when He healed people?

When Jesus went about doing good, healing those who were oppressed of the devil, was He saying that it is *not* God's will to heal? Was Jesus saying that it is only God's will to heal just a few? Certainly not! No! Jesus was demonstrating the Heavenly Father's will to heal people.

God the Father was revealing Himself to man through His Son Jesus to say to mankind: "I am your kind, loving Heavenly Father. Whatever you see Jesus doing, that is My will. In My Word you can see Jesus healing people everywhere He went. Therefore, you can know for certain that it is My will to heal!"

For example, God was personally speaking to us when He spoke through Jesus in Matthew chapter 7.

MATTHEW 7:7-11

7 Ask, and it shall be given you; seek, and ye shall find; knock, and IT SHALL BE OPENED unto you:

8 For every one that asketh receiveth; and he that seeketh findeth; and to him that knocketh IT SHALL BE OPENED.

9 Or what man is there of you, whom if his son ask bread, will he give him a stone?

10 Or if he ask a fish, will he give him a serpent?

11 If ye then, being evil, know how to give good gifts unto your children, HOW MUCH MORE shall your Father which is in heaven give GOOD THINGS to them that ask him?

Jesus was saying, "If you being evil or *natural* know how to give good gifts to your children, *how much more* will your Heavenly Father give good things to those who ask Him?" How much more will God give good things to us!

God the Father is trying to tell us through Jesus that just as a natural father loves his children and desires the best for them, *how much more* does He, our Heavenly Father, love His children and desire to give them good things in life. *How much more!*

For instance, if your child was burning up with fever, how many of you parents would heal him if you could? Certainly you would make your child well if it were in your power to do so. God wants to do the same for His children. And *God is able!*

Someone asked, "If God is able, then why doesn't He just heal every sick person?"

Certainly God is omnipotent or all-powerful. But He can only do in your life what you permit Him to do. God responds to faith.

Some argue that since God is omnipotent, He can make people do anything He wants them to do. But if that were true, then He'd make all sinners get saved, and He'd make all Christians pay their tithes! No, God gave man a free will, and He will not violate people's free will.

But some folks believe, "Well, whatever is God's will, He'll just do it. If it is God's will to heal me, He'll do it. If He doesn't heal me, it must not be His will to heal." But, you see, God can't do any more in your life than you permit Him to do.

Do Your Part
In Receiving God's Blessings

You have a part to play in receiving God's blessings, including healing. For instance, Jesus says, *"Behold, I stand at the door, and knock: if any man hear my voice, and OPEN THE DOOR, I will come in to him, and will sup with him, and he with me"* (Rev. 3:20).

Man is a free moral agent; he has the ability and right to make his own choices in life. He can open the door of his heart and choose to accept

Jesus Christ as Savior and Lord and be born again, or he can choose to reject Jesus.

Even after you are born again, you don't lose your will or your right to choose.

DEUTERONOMY 30:19
19 I call heaven and earth to record this day against you, that I have set before you life and death, blessing and cursing: THEREFORE CHOOSE LIFE, that both thou and thy seed may live.

You make your own choices in this life. Why? Because for one reason, your body is the house *you* — your spirit man — lives in. You are the one in authority over your "house," your own body.

Since you are the one in authority over your own body, you can let God's Word into your heart with its health and healing, or you can let the devil's thoughts and symptoms in with his sickness and disease.

You have a choice about what you will do with God's Word. Will you attend to it? Will you incline your ear to it? Will you keep it before your eyes and in the midst of your heart?

If you do, God's Word will become healing, health, and life to you. It will be a never-failing remedy for all your flesh and for every circumstance of your life. God's Word is always a never-failing remedy for all the problems of life for those who attend to it and put it first place!

Actually, people bring upon themselves much of the trouble they experience in life. And, of course, the devil accommodates them in wrongdoing too. Nearly all the tears that are shed are selfish. If folks would just do what the Bible said, it would save them so much misery.

You can spare yourself a lot of misery in life just by inclining your ear to God's sayings! You need to incline your ear to what God's Word says about every area of your life. And when you obey one part of the Bible, it makes it a whole lot easier to obey other parts of the Bible.

On the other hand, if you disobey God's Word along a particular line, it makes it easier to disobey the Word in other areas. And when you are in disobedience, it opens the door to the devil to try to work in your life. It is just better to listen to God and pay attention to what the Bible says.

We need to incline our ears to *all* of God's Word and let it be the final authority in our lives. God's Word is God Himself speaking to us. You can incline your ear to God's sayings if you want to, or you can close your ears to God's sayings.

If you open your ears to God's sayings, you make it possible for your Heavenly Father to pour out on you the "how much more" that He wants to give you: ". . . *HOW MUCH MORE shall your Father which is in heaven GIVE GOOD THINGS to them that ask him?*" (Matt. 7:11).

Just present your petition before your Heavenly Father and ask in faith! He wants to give you the "how much more"! But He can't until you give Him permission to do so by asking!

How else do you give Him permission? By inclining your ear unto His sayings! By asking Him in faith based on His Word. Then He can pour out His blessings on you. And He will pour them out because He is faithful to His Word.

Satan Is the Oppressor — Jesus Is the Deliverer!

God has spoken to us through His Son, Jesus (Heb. 1:1,2). What else is Jesus saying to us. We saw that in Acts 10:38 that Jesus went about doing good and healing all who were oppressed of the devil.

By healing all those who were oppressed by the devil, Jesus was telling us that Satan is the oppressor. Jesus is the Deliverer. God anointed Jesus with the Holy Ghost and power to be the Deliverer! He is the Healer.

Sometimes you hear people say that life is a mystery. But it is no mystery at all if you will get in the Book that solves all mystery — God's Word. It will unveil any mystery in life to you.

You see, the Holy Ghost is the Teacher. He will lead you into all the truth (John 16:13). Therefore, there is no mystery at all about life. It is simple. Satan is the defiler. Satan is the tormentor. Satan is the one who brings sickness and disease. He is the author of sickness and disease; he is the oppressor and our adversary, the thief and the liar (Acts 10:38; John 10:10; 1 Peter 5:8).

But Jesus comes to deliver us and set us free (John 8:32). It is very easy and simple to see that when you incline your ears to what God says in His Word, the Word frees you from whatever would try to bind you. And when Satan is finally eliminated from the earth, the Bible says, "There will be nothing that will hurt or destroy" (Isa. 11:9; 65:25).

Therefore, anything that hurts or destroys must come from Satan. Satan must be the source, because when he is eliminated, there is nothing that hurts or destroys anymore.

You see, some people read God's Word and still miss the fact that Jesus is the Healer. They think that if they are sick, *God* must have put sickness on them to try to teach them something.

But if you will get into the Word, the Holy Ghost will illuminate your mind and your spirit, and you will see that God is the Healer. You will see that Satan is the one who tries to hurt people with sickness and disease. Satan is the author of sickness and disease, not God.

JOHN 10:10
10 The thief cometh not, but for to STEAL, and to KILL, and to DESTROY: I [Jesus] am come that

**they might have LIFE, and that they might have it
MORE ABUNDANTLY.**

The Bible says we are to incline our ears to
God's sayings. That's how we receive abundant life!
Well, it was Jesus Himself who said that Satan is
the thief that steals, kills, and destroys.

So we know that anything that hurts or
destroys is of Satan, not God. Sickness hurts and
destroys, but God *heals* sickness and disease. God
doesn't put sickness on folks.

According to John 10:10, Jesus came to give us
abundant *life* — not sickness and disease.

I've seen people who are being attacked by sickness and disease say, "Well, God must have put this
on me for some purpose. He probably has some
great, mystical plan in mind. He must be trying to
teach me something."

Bless their darling hearts! Folks who believe
that way are playing right into the devil's hands.
And they are being robbed of the blessings, the healing, and the health that God wants them to enjoy.

God is a healing God! God's will is for you to be
well. He even gave you instructions how to stay
well: "Attend to My words. Incline your ear unto
My sayings. Let My words not depart from your
eyes. Keep them in the midst of your heart. For
they are *life* and *health* to those who find them."

It stands to reason that healing must be God's
will or He wouldn't have told us how we can

receive healing and health for our bodies! If sickness was God's will for His children, then why would God tell us how to get out of His will by getting healed!

No, God made provision for our healing by Jesus' stripes at the Cross of Calvary.

MATTHEW 8:17
17 That it might be fulfilled which was spoken by Esaias the prophet, saying, HIMSELF TOOK OUR INFIRMITIES, and BARE OUR SICKNESSES.

1 PETER 2:24
24 Who his own self bare our sins in his own body on the tree, that we, being dead to sins, should live unto righteousness: BY WHOSE STRIPES YE WERE HEALED.

You see, according to the Word, we are already healed by the stripes of Jesus. First Peter 2:24 says, ". . . *by whose stripes YE WERE HEALED.*" That's a past-tense fact in the mind of God!

Therefore, healing and health are God's will for us — not sickness and disease. Now we just need to receive the healing of our bodies that has already been provided for us through Jesus.

People who don't believe it is God's will to heal have a distorted mental picture of the character and nature of God. And the only way they can change that is to get into God's Word — the never-failing remedy! They must incline their ears to

God's Word so they can see what their Heavenly Father is really like.

If they will listen to what the Word says, they will get the right picture of God in their hearts and minds, and their spiritual viewpoint will change; it will no longer be distorted.

Just remember, God's Word is a never-failing *remedy* for all your flesh. If God gave you His Word as a remedy for sickness and disease, why would He want you to go on being sick?

No, God wants you to have abundant life, healing, and health in every area of your life. That's why He gave you His Word to be a never-failing *remedy* for every problem and circumstance you will ever face in life.

Chapter 3
God's Word Is God's Will

God's Word is God's will; it is medicine, and it is health to our flesh. Well, if God's Word is medicine, then it stands to reason that God wants His people to take their medicine so they can get well and stay well.

God tells us exactly how to receive health for all our flesh. He said, "My words are life unto those that find them, and health to all their flesh" (Prov. 4:22).

And God explicitly states right here in His Word that He wants us to find His Word so we can receive *health* for all our flesh. Health is for anyone who finds God's Word. Therefore, healing is God's will for everyone.

MATTHEW 8:1-3
1 When he [Jesus] was come down from the mountain, great multitudes followed him.
2 And, behold, there came a leper and worshipped him, saying, Lord, IF THOU WILT, thou canst make me clean.
3 And Jesus put forth his hand, and touched him, saying, I WILL; be thou clean. And immediately his leprosy was cleansed.

Now incline your ear to His sayings. The "I will" that Jesus said to this leper is also what God the Father is speaking to you about your healing. Jesus said, ". . . *the words that I speak unto you I speak not of myself: but the Father that dwelleth in me, he doeth the works*" (John 14:10).

So what did Jesus say to this leper about healing? Incline your ear unto Jesus' sayings because Jesus is revealing the Father's will on healing too. When Jesus said, "*I WILL; be thou clean,*" He was revealing that it is God's will to heal.

Read through the four Gospels carefully and underline every time Jesus said something about healing. You won't find even one single time where Jesus said, "I *won't* heal you." Not one single time!

Also, notice that the leper believed Jesus *could* heal him, but he questioned whether or not Jesus *would* heal him. The leper said, ". . . *Lord, IF THOU WILT, thou canst make me clean*" (Matt. 8:2).

Remember the Bible said, "Jesus is the Author and Finisher of our faith" (Heb. 12:2). So Jesus completed the leper's faith and settled the issue once and for all about His will to heal when He plainly answered, "I will."

The leper showed his doubt and unbelief by saying, "*If* thou wilt." Many folks today follow the leper's *doubt* rather than Jesus' *willingness* to heal.

If God said, "I will" about healing one person, then He is saying, "I will" about healing *all* people because He is not a respecter of persons (Acts 10:34).

And from Genesis to Revelation, we see God's "I will" to heal, deliver, and set people free. It is sad that people would rather follow the leper's doubt than they would Jesus' faith.

The Centurion's Great Faith

Matthew 8 has more to say about God's willingness to heal. It also shows us what God considers to be great faith. Great faith is reliance on the Word apart from natural circumstances that contradict the Word.

Incline your ear to what God is saying about healing in these verses. You will see that the centurion's servant was healed because of what the centurion *said* — the words he spoke.

The words you speak can determine whether or not you will ever receive your healing. Why? Because your words indicate your faith.

MATTHEW 8:5-10,13
5 And when Jesus was entered into Capernaum, there came unto him a centurion, beseeching him,
6 And saying, Lord, my servant lieth at home sick of the palsy, grievously tormented.
7 And Jesus saith unto him, I WILL come and HEAL him.
8 The centurion answered and said, Lord, I am

> **not worthy that thou shouldest come under my
> roof: BUT SPEAK THE WORD ONLY, and my ser-
> vant shall be healed.**
> **9 For I am a man under authority, having soldiers
> under me: and I say to this man, Go, and he goeth;
> and to another, Come, and he cometh; and to my
> servant, Do this, and he doeth it.**
> **10 When Jesus heard it, he marvelled, and said to
> them that followed, Verily I say unto you, I HAVE
> NOT FOUND SO GREAT FAITH, no, not in Israel....**
> **13 And Jesus said unto the centurion, GO THY
> WAY; AND AS THOU HAST BELIEVED, SO BE IT
> DONE UNTO THEE. And his servant was healed in
> the selfsame hour.**

What did Jesus say to the centurion about healing his servant? Again, Jesus said, "I *will* heal
him." He didn't say, "I won't heal him." And He's
never said, "I won't" to anyone who believed Him
and came to Him in faith to be healed.

You'll notice that the centurion's answer was
full of faith. His words demonstrated his faith. He
said to Jesus, ". . . *SPEAK THE WORD ONLY, and
my servant shall be healed*" (v. 8).

The centurion inclined his ear unto Jesus' sayings! Then the centurion spoke words in line with
Jesus' sayings. And Jesus called the words that the
centurion spoke — *great faith*!

Well, what is great faith? The ingredient to great
faith is found in the centurion's answer: ". . . *SPEAK
THE WORD ONLY* . . . *.*" Great faith is simply
faith in God's Word. It is taking God at His Word.

Great faith is speaking God's Word in faith and acting like the Word is so.

God wants us to have the same great faith in His Word that the centurion had in Jesus' words. God wants us to have confidence in the authority and integrity of His Word.

Because of the centurion's great faith, Jesus could say to him, ". . . *Go thy way; and as thou hast believed, so be it done unto thee . . ."* (v. 13). And the centurion's servant was healed in the same hour.

Jesus is saying to each of us today: "Go your way; and as you have *believed,* so be it done unto you." Just go your way, and what you are believing God for will be done unto you as long as you are acting on God's Word in faith.

The Bible says God never changes (Mal. 3:6; Heb. 13:8). What He has done for anyone else, He will do for you if you will believe Him and take Him at His Word.

As I said, God doesn't favor one person over another because He is not a respecter of persons. But God does favor anyone who is committed to believing His Word and acting on it.

God told us in Proverbs 4:20 to attend to His words, and incline our ears unto His sayings. The benefit and result of inclining your ear to God's Word is great faith. Great faith receives healing, health, and life.

Jesus Is Willing To Heal Everyone

Then Jesus said, "The words that I speak unto you, they are the words of the Father." So if you want to hear God the Father speaking, listen to Jesus! Since we know Jesus said that God the Father is willing to heal (Matt 8:3,7), then what else is Jesus saying?

> **MATTHEW 8:14-17**
> 14 And when Jesus was come into Peter's house, he saw his wife's mother laid, and sick of a fever.
> 15 And he TOUCHED HER HAND, and THE FEVER LEFT HER: and she arose, and ministered unto them.
> 16 When the even was come, they brought unto him MANY that were possessed with devils: and he cast out the spirits with his word, and healed ALL that were sick:
> 17 That it might be fulfilled which was spoken by Esaias the prophet, saying, HIMSELF TOOK OUR INFIRMITIES, and BARE OUR SICKNESSES.

There are many truths in these verses that can be expounded upon. But I think one great truth that outshines the rest is God's willingness to heal *everyone*.

For example, in verses 14 and 15, we read that Jesus healed Peter's mother-in-law. Now many people believe it is God's will to heal *some* people or a selected few, such as one of the relatives of Jesus' disciples. But they don't believe it is God's will to heal *everyone*.

But notice that the same day Jesus healed Peter's mother-in-law, He also healed *all* those who needed healing. The Bible says that same day many were delivered and Jesus ". . . *healed ALL that were sick*" (v. 16).

That means Jesus healed everyone in that crowd who was sick. Why did Jesus heal the multitudes? Listen to the sayings of God's Word. Jesus healed them *"That it might be fulfilled which was spoken by Esaias the prophet, saying, Himself took our infirmities, and bare our sicknesses"* (Matt. 8:17).

Jesus was moved by compassion to heal the sick (Matt. 9:36). His earthly ministry was the will of God in action on behalf of man (John 5:19,30,36; 8:28,29; Acts 10:38). Therefore, healing *is* God's will!

So we can see from Matthew 8:16 that healing does not just belong to a selected few. God doesn't favor some and not others.

I thoroughly believe that is why this account of Jesus healing Peter's mother-in-law is put right next to the account of His healing the *multitudes* — *all* those who were sick.

Otherwise, people would try to read Matthew 8:17: "Himself bore Peter's mother-in-law's infirmity and bare *her* sickness." Or "Jesus bore *some* people's infirmity and sickness."

But the Bible doesn't say that. No, God is no respecter of persons. If He healed one person, He will heal another. Just take Him at His Word.

Incline your ears unto God's sayings! What is God the Father saying? He is saying that the sickness and infirmity of us *all* were laid on Jesus. Therefore, we can *all* be healed!

MATTHEW 8:17
17 That it might be fulfilled which was spoken by Esaias the prophet, saying, HIMSELF TOOK OUR INFIRMITIES, and BARE OUR SICKNESSES.

It was on the basis of this truth that Jesus healed the multitudes. Incline your ears unto God's sayings! The Bible contains God's sayings. Since Jesus healed "*all* those who were sick" who came to Him in faith, if you are sick in your body, just come to Him right now in faith and receive your healing!

God Wants To Heal *You!*

I've been in the healing ministry for more than sixty years now, and I have found that the biggest hindrance to getting people healed is to convince them that it is God's will to heal them.

Many Christians make some effort to approach God and receive healing, yet many times the thought lurks in the back of their minds, *I know God does heal people, but it might not be His will to heal me.*

But, you see, these folks aren't inclining their ears unto God's sayings. When you incline your ear to what God says, you *know* the will of God concerning healing. Over and over again God's willingness to heal is expressed in the pages of His Word.

Let's listen to God's Word continually and incline our ears unto *His* sayings. As we incline our ears to His sayings, that Word will get deep into our heart, and we will know that "by His stripes we were healed."

I've said many times that just because I ate one T-bone steak doesn't mean I'm never going to eat another one.

It is the same way with the Word. In the natural, continually feeding your *body* with good food keeps it strong. And in the supernatural realm, continually feeding your *spirit* with God's Word keeps your spirit strong and your faith alive. Actually, the Word feeds your faith.

When you feed your spirit on God's Word along the lines of healing, you are building health and healing into your body, because God's Word is a never-failing remedy. It is health to all your flesh!

In every situation and circumstance of life, ask yourself, *What does God's Word say?* Then feed your faith along that line. When you get your faith built up in the subject of healing, results will be forthcoming.

If you will put God's Word first, life can be different for you. God's Word is life, health, and a never-failing remedy in every area of life.

Chapter 4
Healing Is the Children's Bread

We are to incline our ears to God's sayings so we can have life and health. In His earth walk, Jesus was the will of God in action to bring *life* and *health* to people. Therefore, what else did Jesus say about healing?

Jesus said that healing is the children's bread. That means healing *belongs* to the children of God. Your Heavenly Father already provided it for you.

MATTHEW 15:21-28
21 Then Jesus went thence, and departed into the coasts of Tyre and Sidon.
22 And, behold, a woman of Canaan came out of the same coasts, and cried unto him, saying, Have mercy on me, O Lord, thou son of David; my daughter is grievously vexed with a devil.
23 But he answered her not a word. And his disciples came and besought him, saying, Send her away; for she crieth after us.
24 But he answered and said, I am not sent but unto the lost sheep of the house of Israel.
25 Then came she and worshipped him, saying, Lord, help me.
26 But he answered and said, It is not meet to take the CHILDREN'S BREAD, and to cast it to dogs.
27 And she said, Truth, Lord: yet the dogs eat of

**the crumbs which fall from their masters' table.
28 Then Jesus answered and said unto her, O
woman, GREAT IS THY FAITH: be it unto thee
even as thou wilt. And HER DAUGHTER WAS
MADE WHOLE from that very hour.**

Healing is the children's bread! If healing is the
children's bread, then if you are born again, healing is *your* bread. These are Jesus' own words!
Therefore, healing belongs to you right now. Just
receive what belongs to you. You can incline your
ear to the fact that healing is your bread because
Jesus Himself said it.

If you are born again, then you are God's child,
and healing has already been provided for you! It
would help you to say out loud: "Healing belongs to
me. It is my daily bread! I can partake of my daily
bread right *now!*"

Some of you need to incline your ear unto that
and say it until it registers on the inside of you, in
your spirit. The Word won't work for you if it is just
in your head. But when the Word gets on the
inside of you in your heart, then results are forthcoming!

So healing is the children's bread. Healing is a
provision that belongs to you from your Heavenly
Father like bread belongs to a child from his
earthly father. But healing also belongs to you
based on other rights and privileges of your blood-
bought inheritance in Christ.

Healing Is Your Family Right

Healing is also your family right because when you became a child of God, you became a part of the family of God. The Bible says, ". . . *ye have received the Spirit of adoption, whereby we cry, Abba, Father*" (Rom. 8:15). God is your very own Heavenly Father. Therefore, healing belongs to you because you are God's own child.

If you have been born again and belong in God's family, then you don't have to wait for what belongs to you. Receive healing right now! It's yours because healing is the children's bread. You are God's child, so healing belongs to you by right of your inheritance in God's family. Healing is your bread, so partake right now of what belongs to you!

Healing Is Your Legal Right

Healing is your legal right because the New Covenant is a legal document sealed by the blood of Jesus (Heb. 8:6; 12:24; 13:20). The New Covenant guarantees you everything that Jesus secured for you at the Cross, which includes divine healing (Matt. 8:17; 1 Peter 2:24).

Legally, Jesus suffered on the Cross as your Substitute, so you could be free from the sickness and disease that would try to attack your body. Therefore, you have a *legal right* to divine healing through the new and better covenant ratified by Jesus' blood (Heb. 8:6).

Healing Is Your Redemptive Right

Healing is also your redemptive right because it is included in God's redemptive plan. Jesus provided divine healing on the Cross of Calvary in His death, burial, and resurrection.

> **ISAIAH 53:4,5**
> **4 Surely he hath BORNE OUR GRIEFS** [sickness and disease], **and CARRIED OUR SORROWS** [pain]: **yet we did esteem him stricken, smitten of God, and afflicted.**
> **5 But he was wounded for our transgressions, he was bruised for our iniquities: the chastisement of our peace was upon him; and WITH HIS STRIPES WE ARE HEALED.**

Jesus purchased our healing for us just as He provided remission of our sins. Therefore, we also have a *redemptive right* to divine healing. Every born-again child of God has the right to receive healing based on Jesus' redemptive work on the Cross.

> **1 PETER 2:24**
> **24 Who his own self bare our sins IN HIS OWN BODY ON THE TREE, that we, being dead to sins, should live unto righteousness: BY WHOSE STRIPES YE WERE HEALED.**

> **MATTHEW 8:17**
> **17 That it might be fulfilled which was spoken by Esaias the prophet, saying, HIMSELF TOOK OUR INFIRMITIES, and BARE OUR SICKNESSES.**

Since Jesus bore our sickness and infirmities for us, we don't need to bear them! Don't continue to bear what Jesus already bore for you on the Cross of Calvary.

Healing Is Your Prayerful Right

Healing is your prayerful right because God said, ". . . *What things soever ye desire, WHEN YE PRAY, believe that ye receive them, and ye shall have them*" (Mark 11:24). It is your right to claim your healing in the Name of Jesus.

PHILIPPIANS 4:19
19 But my God shall supply ALL YOUR NEED according to his riches in glory by Christ Jesus.

Healing is also something we need and desire. Because we need it, God provided it for us. After all, God promised to meet all of our needs. If you desire healing for your body, claim it in Jesus' Name based on the Word of God.

Healing for your body is a desire, isn't it? God is the One who promised to satisfy your desires that are in line with His Word. He said, ". . . *What things soever ye desire, when ye pray, believe that ye receive them, and ye shall have them*" (Mark 11:24). Go ahead and receive your healing right now!

God in His great redemptive plan provided quickening and healing for our mortal bodies by the power of the Holy Spirit.

ROMANS 8:11
11 But if the Spirit of him that raised up Jesus

from the dead dwell in you, he that raised up Christ from the dead SHALL ALSO QUICKEN [make alive] YOUR MORTAL BODIES by his Spirit that dwelleth in you.

When you pray, you can appropriate what you need by faith in God's Word. Bring your request boldly before God's throne of grace (Heb. 4:16). You have a right to prayerfully appropriate or receive divine healing!

Healing Is Your Divine Right

Healing is our divine right because it belongs to us and was given to us by our divine Heavenly Father. The Bible says that when we were born again, we became new creatures (2 Cor. 5:17). We became the sons of God (Rom. 8:14,16).

It is the life of God coming into our spirit that makes us new creatures. We are born of God's Spirit in the new birth (John 3:3-8). We were created anew in the image and likeness of God in our spirits. Therefore, we have a divine right to healing.

Healing Is Your Provision Right

Healing is your provision because God gave it to you at His table of provision.

PSALM 23:5
5 Thou PREPAREST A TABLE BEFORE ME in the presence of mine enemies. . . .

Who are our enemies? Satan and his host. Demons and evil spirits that would try to put sickness and disease on us. The Bible calls Satan our adversary (1 Peter 5:8).

But what is on God's table of provision that's been well prepared for *us*? The children's bread! Healing is the children's bread, and it is already on your Heavenly Father's table of provision just waiting for you to partake of it. So just ask your Heavenly Father, "Father, please pass the bread!"

Your Heavenly Father has prepared a table of blessing for you, and it includes healing for your body! Healing is always on the Master's table. The Master is calling you to take your place and come and dine at His banqueting table so you can enjoy what He's already provided for you.

You see, feeding on what God's Word has to say about healing is like eating food in the natural. Jesus said in Matthew 4:4: ". . . *Man shall not live by bread alone, but by every word that proceedeth out of the mouth of God.*" Bread just stands for food. Therefore, God's Word on healing is your bread.

In other words, when you analyze what Jesus said, He is saying that what food is to the body, the Word of God is to our spirit. You need to feed on God's Word in the area of healing. Healing is the children's bread and feeding on God's Word on healing can make you whole in every area of your life!

Chapter 5
Success Is Found In the Word

The answer to everything you need in life, including healing, can be found in God's holy written Word. It's what you do with God's Word that determines your success or failure in life.

God's Word is life and health to all your flesh, and it's a never-failing remedy in all the affairs of life. But you'll have to incline your ear to it and apply it before the Word will benefit you.

Every time I teach about God's Word being a remedy, I am reminded of a testimony I heard during a meeting I held in Albuquerque, New Mexico.

After one of the services, a woman approached my wife and me to talk to us. Pointing to her feet, this woman blurted out, "I'm forty-seven years old, and this is the first pair of shoes I've ever had on in my life!"

My wife and I both looked at her feet, and we could see that she was wearing a new pair of shoes. But we could have interpreted what she said a number of different ways. Did she mean that when she was forty-seven years old, she finally got enough money together to buy a new pair of shoes?

The woman went on to explain. She said: "I was born with a crippled foot, so I'd never worn a pair of shoes in my life. One foot was normal, so I could wear one shoe, but I've always had to wear a specially made shoe on my deformed foot.

"Also, one leg was smaller and shorter than the other one, so I hardly ever went out in public because I was always trying to hide my condition.

"But then someone gave me a set of your tapes on faith, Brother Hagin. I started listening to those tapes, and at first I couldn't get a thing in the world out of them. But I just kept on listening to them over and over again."

She said, "I had been anointed with oil and prayed for many times. Every evangelist who came to our church would anoint me with oil, lay hands on me, and pray for me.

"But this time, no one anointed me with oil. No one laid hands on me. No one prayed for me. In fact, I didn't even pray myself."

She said, "But after about six months of listening to your tapes almost nonstop, my foot and leg just began to straighten out. Now they are completely normal!"

Then she added, "Also, I was born without a little toe on my deformed foot, but God even grew a little toe on that foot!"

Somebody may say, "I don't believe that!"

Well, if you don't believe it, then it won't work for you. You'll just need to incline your ear unto God's sayings until faith arises in your heart. Then you can believe God for the impossible too.

How did this woman become well and whole? Just by inclining her ear unto God's sayings. Remember, "My words are health and healing to all your flesh" — to your body (Prov. 4:22). And Jesus said, "My words are spirit and they are life" (John 6:63).

The Word Produces Results

This woman wasn't healed because someone prayed for her. Don't misunderstand me; I'm not belittling prayer. Prayer is right and thoroughly scriptural. We know that from the Bible.

But notice what Proverbs 4:20-22 says again. Notice that it doesn't say a word about prayer. It only talks about attending to the Word; inclining your ear to the Word; not departing from the Word; and keeping the Word in the midst of your heart. When you do that, then God's Word will be life and health to your body.

PROVERBS 4:20-22
20 My son, ATTEND to my words; INCLINE thine ear unto my sayings.
21 Let them NOT DEPART from thine eyes; KEEP them in the midst of thine heart.

**22 For they are LIFE unto those that find them,
and HEALTH to all their FLESH** [body].

Therefore, as scriptural as prayer is, this Scripture does not say one word about praying! Of course God answers prayer. But these Scriptures aren't saying you have to pray to put God's Word to work for you. Healing can work for you just by putting the Word to work for you.

Proverbs 4:20-22 tells us exactly how to put the Word to work for you: Attend to God's Words. Incline your ear to His sayings. Let them not depart from before your eyes. Keep the Word in the midst of your heart. That's when the healing power in God's Word will show up in your flesh!

This woman found out that if she would do what the Word said, the Word would work for her! She inclined her ear to God's Word, and the Word she heard for six months got into her spirit and began working in her body. It began quickening and making alive her mortal body (Rom. 8:11).

Just by inclining her ear to God's Word, her foot grew out and her leg straightened up. For the first time in her life, her foot and leg were normal, and the Word did it all! Her body became completely well and normal just from inclining her ear to God's Word and hiding it in her heart.

I have often thought, What if this woman had quit listening to those tapes after the third or fourth time? Or what would have happened if she had quit listening after just three months?

What if she had given up, saying, "I'm just not getting anything out of this"? If she had stopped inclining her ear unto God's sayings, she wouldn't have experienced healing, health, and life in her body!

You see, very often, our problem is that we've seen God work miracles and we've even seen the supernatural demonstrations of His power, so we wait for Him to do something spectacular.

And sometimes God does move spectacularly in healings and miracles. But His Word works all the time — and it is just as supernatural! And if we'll just incline our ear to what it is saying, the results can be just as spectacular.

In other words, we can't guarantee that there will always be gifts of healings or the gift of miracles in manifestation because they are manifested as the Spirit wills (1 Cor. 12:11). We can't guarantee that the gift of special faith will be in manifestation to bring about a healing or a cure.

But I'll tell you one thing we can guarantee! Actually, God Himself guarantees it (Isa. 55:11). His Word will always work for you — every single day and in every single circumstance. Glory to God! The Word always works.

That's why we constantly preach and teach the Word. We're trying to get people to incline their ear to God's sayings. If they'll just keep the Word in their heart, God Himself guarantees that the Word works (Num. 23:19; Matt. 24:35).

Why? Because God stands as the authority behind every word spoken in His Word (Ps. 138:2). That's the reason He said, "Attend to My words." He knows that His Word won't fail!

This woman's healing came about because she inclined her ear to what God said. She put God's Word to work in her situation. God's words are spirit and they are life (John 6:63).

Irrefutable Proof

I like to check up on testimonies I hear. The Word is an infallible proof, but I also like to check up in the natural realm too. And the Bible does say, *"Prove all things; hold fast that which is good"* (1 Thess. 5:21).

This woman who had been crippled told us, "Some people you know used to be my pastors. I know that because you mentioned their names on those tapes I listened to."

"Who?" I asked.

She said, "Brother and Sister Goodwin."

At that time the Goodwins were pastors of the First Assembly of God church in Pasadena, Texas. Both of them have gone on to be with the Lord now.

We said, "Oh, yes, they're good friends of ours."

Well, some time after we talked to this woman, my wife and I saw the Goodwins. My wife began to talk to Sister Goodwin about this woman. When my wife mentioned her name, immediately Sister Goodwin said, "Oh, yes! The little crippled girl."

Brother and Sister Goodwin first met this woman back in the '30s when the woman was just a girl.

My wife said, "Well, she's not crippled now. We saw her. She's perfectly healed."

Sister Goodwin said, "She was crippled when we were her pastors. In fact, her mother told us that she was born that way."

You see, here is irrefutable proof that she was crippled, but that by inclining her ear to God's sayings, she was totally healed!

Of course, receiving healing through your own faith in God's Word is not the only way to be healed. But it is one of the best ways because then you learn how to put the Word to work for you anytime you need it.

Once you learn that there's power in God's Word to heal you, spiritually you are a long way down the road! That means you've found out that God will work for you through His Word every single time.

PSALMS 107:20
20 HE SENT HIS WORD, AND HEALED THEM,
and delivered them from their destructions.

Dr. John G. Lake once said something interesting about healing. He said that sometimes our instant healings are a curse to us because people get healed instantly and go away and forget. It's like the ten lepers. Only one of them returned to give thanks unto the Lord.

But when people are healed gradually, they learn that it's as they walk by faith in the Word that they get better and better and start improving. They learn how to make the Word work for them. They also learn great spiritual lessons that work for them the rest of their lives.

Now that was Lake's opinion, but there's a lot of truth to those statements. But before you can put the Word to work for you, you'll need to continually incline your ear unto God's sayings. Then God's Word can be a remedy for you anytime you need it.

You see, when you are walking in the Word, you are walking in health. When you are walking in the Word, you are walking in healing and life. When you are walking in the Word, the Word is working for you, and it will produce health, healing, and life.

When the Word is working in you, you are full of life. It stands to reason that when you are filled with the Word, you will be healthy and strong.

God's Word — The Remedy

The answer to every adversity of life can be found in the pages of God's holy written Word.

God's Word is life and health to all our flesh. God's Word is a never-failing remedy in every situation and circumstance you will ever face in life.

I get more thrilled teaching healing from Proverbs 4:20-22 than I do from any other standpoint, because this is the way I was healed and raised up from a deathbed as a teenager.

I had a deformed heart and an incurable blood disease from birth and never ran and played as a child like the other little children did. I used to sit inside and watch from the window in awe as other children ran and laughed and played outside. I didn't have a normal childhood.

Then I became totally bedfast. I know what it means to lie there bedfast sixteen long months. That's a long time to be in bed. I couldn't even turn over on my side; my folks had to turn me over using a sheet. Someone had to feed me, too, because I couldn't feed myself.

I was alive on the inside, but it seemed like I was trapped in a cage because my body was paralyzed. It was a terrible ordeal. It's almost impossible to describe what it was like to lie there on a deathbed paralyzed for those sixteen long months, just staring at the ceiling, knowing I was going to die.

I know what it's like to have no hope for a better tomorrow. When it was daytime, you wished it was night. And when it was nighttime, you wished it was day.

I've been there when the doctors shook their head and said, "We can't do anything for you. You'll just have to die." Five doctors told me that!

I know what people are going through who are dealing with sickness and disease in their bodies because I've experienced that too.

While sickness and disease ravaged my body, I would just stare at the ceiling hour after hour, day after day, wishing more than anything else just to be able to live. I agonized as I searched my mind for answers. I knew there had to be an answer somewhere.

I know what it's like when the sun shines brightly outside, but the room where I was imprisoned by sickness and disease was filled with darkness and death.

Death hung like a shadow of gloom over my bed as I lay there and planned my own funeral. I was only a teenager. I hadn't even begun to live, yet medical science said I had to die.

I've been there when death was imminent. People asked me, "Son, who do you want to preach your funeral? What songs do you want sung?"

I've been there when there was no hope and people asked me, "Who do you want to be your pallbearers?" I know what it's like to suffer like that, knowing I had to die. I've been there.

But, glory to God, I also know what it's like when the light of God's Word comes shining in! Oh, thank God, I've been there too!

The Psalmist said, *"The entrance of thy words giveth light; it giveth understanding unto the simple"* (Ps. 119:130). It was the entrance of God's Word that gave me light! The Word became my remedy.

But, you see, God's words can't find entrance until you incline your ear to His sayings! Then His words will give you light and direct your path.

When I was lying on that deathbed, I knew some way or another that my answer was in God's Word. At first I couldn't even understand the Bible; I just couldn't figure it out. But I kept reading it because I knew my answer was somewhere in the Word.

I'd gotten hold of Mark 11:24 when I first became bedfast. But I didn't know what it meant, and I didn't know how to make it work for me.

MARK 11:24
24 Therefore I say unto you, What things soever ye desire, when ye pray, believe that ye receive them, and ye shall have them.

So in the nighttime as I lay dying, I just began repeating that verse over and over again, sometimes all night long. I did that thousands of times, many times all night long.

At first, Mark 11:24 was just words to me. But I knew that some way or another there was healing for me in that verse. And finally the light shone through, and the truth of God's Word dawned on my heart.

I kept inclining my ear to God's sayings! God's Word began working in my body like medicine. And finally I received healing from the top of my head to the soles of my feet. I got up off that deathbed completely well, and I've been well ever since!

"Yes, Brother Hagin," someone said, "that happened to you because God called you to preach."

But Mark 11:24 didn't work for me because God called me to preach. It doesn't say that Scripture just works for preachers. It worked for me because I inclined my ear to God's sayings. And it will work for you, too, if you will put God's Word first above every situation and circumstance that comes your way.

Put God's Word first in your life. Take your medicine. Then watch the Word become your remedy. Life can be different for you.

You don't have to go through life suffering with sickness and disease. If you are struggling today with the tests and trials of life, stop struggling and start inclining! In fact, no matter what test or trial you may be facing, God's Word is a never-failing remedy!